BUSINESS GUIDE AND EMPLOYMENT ROLE

BUSINESS GUIDE AND EMPLOYMENT ROLE

CIDI MAHAMMED

AuthorHouse™ UK Ltd.
1663 Liberty Drive
Bloomington, IN 47403 USA
www.authorhouse.co.uk
Phone: 0800.197.4150

© 2014 Cidi Mahammed. All rights reserved.

No part of this book may be reproduced, stored in a retrieval system, or transmitted by any means without the written permission of the author.

Published by AuthorHouse 09/30/2014

ISBN: 978-1-4969-9250-5 (sc)
ISBN: 978-1-4969-9253-6 (e)

Any people depicted in stock imagery provided by Thinkstock are models, and such images are being used for illustrative purposes only.
Certain stock imagery © Thinkstock.

This book is printed on acid-free paper.

Because of the dynamic nature of the Internet, any web addresses or links contained in this book may have changed since publication and may no longer be valid. The views expressed in this work are solely those of the author and do not necessarily reflect the views of the publisher, and the publisher hereby disclaims any responsibility for them.

CONTENTS

PART ONE 1

- The Economic Background 5
- Observing The Economic System..6
- Looking At The Economy In Total 7
- Looking At The Economy In Unitary Basis 8
- National Management Policies 9
- Finance Management...10
- Cash Management..11
- The Balance Of Payment Account...12
- Managing The Balance Of Payment 13
- Contribution Of Enterprise In Economic Activity..............14
- Contribution Of Business Corporation Towards Growth..... 15
- Economic Growth As A Motivation
  For Business Enterprise 16
- The Contribution Of Business Enterprise
  In Promoting Welfare..17
- Business Activities Aim At Improving Overall Welfare 19
- Business Strategy Aim At Economic Development 20
- The Aggregate Observation Of The Economy For Welfare 22
- The Solitary Observation Of The Economy For Wellbeing.... 23
- The Monetary Institutions..24
- The Monetary Institutional Framework 25
- The Influence Of Financial Institutions 26
- The Collective Contribution Of Banks................................. 27
- The Single Contribution Of Monetary Institutions............ 28
- The Strategic Aims Of The Financial Institutions 29

- The Objectives Of The Monetary Institutions For Wellbeing 30
- The Market For Consumer Goods And Services 31
- The Market Environment 33
- Looking At Consumer Behaviour 34
- Considering The Supply Of Goods And Services 36
- Business plans Aim At Meeting Customer Demand 37
- Business Plans For Producers Of Goods And Services 38
- The Price Of Goods And Services 39
- The Equilibrium Price 40
- A Bargain Price 41
- The Contribution Of Business In Stabilising The Market 42
- The Importance Of The Economic System For Business 43
- The Important Of The Financial Institution For Business 44
- The Importance Of Business Operation For Economy 46
- The Importance Of The Market For Business Enterprising 47
- Excel Economy For Welfare 48
- Excellent Business Enterprising 49

PART TWO 51

- Business Organisations 55
- Solitary Business Organisation 57
- Combined Business Organisations 58
- The Formation Of Companies 59
- Companies Limited By Shares 60
- Companies Limited By Guarantee 62
- Other forms Of Business Organisations 63
- Charitable Organisations 64
- Business Legal Framework 65
- Budgetary measures For Business 66
- Tax Planning For Businesses 67
- Reporting Financial Performance For Business 68
- The Audit Of Business Entity 70
- Managing Business Finance 71

- Corporate Management Of Business Entities 73
- The Assessment Of Business Performance 75
- The Style And Structure Of Business Organisations 77
- The Business Organisational Environment 78
- The Sustainability Of Industrial Business 79
- The Economic Motivation For Business 80
- The Social Motivation For Business 81
- The Regulation Of Business Industry 82
- The Contribution Of Business Organisation 83
- The Contribution Of Business
  For Economic Development 84

PART THREE 85

- Employment Role 89
- Employees In The Economy 90
- Employers In The Economy 91
- Contract Of Employment 92
- Contract For Employment 93
- The Manner Of Good Team Work 94
- The Manner Of Good Interpersonal Relation 95
- The Manner Of Safe And Secure Environment 96
- The Manner Of Clean Environment 97
- The Management Panel 98
- A Variety Of Team Managers 99
- The Engagement In Continuing
  Professional Development Programme 100
- Productivity In Employment 102
- The Provision Of Benefit In Employment 103
- The Benefit Of Engaging In Employment Role 104
- The Benefit Of Employment For The Economy 106

PROFILE

Business studies were my favourite aspect in our school learning curriculum. In school days I specialises on this aspect of the education and learning curriculum. And leaving school and embarking on professional business education and learning programme, have acquired me this immense knowledge in production of this material guide. Being a member of a business professional body, have develop my skills in understanding the concept of business and the influence this have in relation to the economy.

Being a member of a professional body, have place me on footing in embarking on extensive continuing professional development courses. These learning programme have put me in better position, in improving my skills with regard my career. And this have develop my knowledge and understanding of the concept of business and economic affairs. Doing continued professional development learning programme have prove beneficial, through improve work methods in the business working environment. These continuing professional development programme have earn me vital techniques, in understanding about business management and methods.

In work environment also continued participation in playing a role in employment, have as such acquired me some essential experience in need for the development of my knowledge and understanding about business concept and economic affairs. Continued engagement in this way as such have played a crucial role in developing my techniques in understanding about business methods and management policies. Playing a role in employment and taking duties in various role in the organisation and the business environment, have lead me in knowing the way of business and economic affairs.

Current affairs too have played a significant role in giving me an exposure to the business and economic environment. This way of participation in the mass media, have giving me an immense exposure to the business and economic environment. The continued participation in business and economic programmes in the media have as such giving this exposure. The business and economic environment is shape every day, through the mass media. So an exposure to this world can provide some crucial insight in the way business and economic affairs in done in the economy.

More also as a business practitioner, have as such contribute towards my skills and techniques acquired in producing this material guide. Working with business owners and providing help in the progress for doing business, have as such acquired me some experience. And this too as such have contribute in understanding the business and economic environment.

Every day as such is an engagement in business of some form. And in this respect have place me in good position in knowing more about the environment of business and economic issues that influence our daily lives. The passion and desires too in this subject matter, have serve as contributory factor in the production of this material guide. Business and economic affairs is as such very influential in our daily lives. So a passion and desires in this respect have develop my techniques in understanding about business methods and management.

PREFACE

Making reference to business and playing a role in employment, places more value than any in our lives today. In today's environment and in particular in modern economies today, business adventure is quite a significant aspect in our living. Virtually our lives can be made no better, without business adventure. Business is thus seen as such as a major aspect in our daily lives. In today's present, many people are engage in business adventure, of one kind to another. This is so in order that, individual in particular can place themselves in some adventure of a kind, so as to meet their ends, in order to support one daily living. And so the drive for this being that, one may desire to engage oneself in this kind, so that one can be place in a better position for improve wellbeing. Individuals in our local environment participate in different sets of business adventure. The motivation for this being to realise some gain for so participation. So as such entrepreneurs engage themselves in business, as a result of profit motive in so doing. So suppose one suppose oneself, what is the motivation for doing business, obviously an answer to this, is that for one to realise some profit from engagement. Thus individuals do business to realise some profit, so as to make some form of compensation for so participation. Profit realisation is as such a significant aspect for doing business. People are in business so that some profit can be realise, as a way of reward in participation of this kind. The profit realise in business represent a crucial and form the vital sum for extraction from the business. Business profit is that aspect of the stake in business, that can set aside some income for realisation for the owners of capital in the venture. The profit can be use for instance to pay dividend to the owners of capital of the business, or say some is plug back in to the business, to make more room for expansion. Single businessmen in the local environment today engage themselves in business, say as a self employed. So in this regard this is their only employment and they participate in this way of business, so as to realise some gain in return. And so the profit from this venture, can serve and represent the wages as a reward to the owner of the business. This is equally applicable to partnership businesses as well. For companies and corporation the business may be separate from the owners of the business. Wealthy individuals in the economy invest in these companies so as to realise some gain. And so the profit from operation can set aside some income to distribute back to these investors, so as to compensate them for the capital employed in the business.

Furthermore in our economies today employment is quite a significant aspect in our lives. People go about every day in search for employment opportunities. The motivation for this being that individuals want to gain themselves some income in this way of economic participation. Seeking employment is thus essential for improve wellbeing. Peoples life can be promoted of some sort as a result for taking employment. Depending on skills and capability one can earn crucial sums of money, as a result of taking employment. So in this regard individuals in our economies today are engage in different sets of ways, in playing role of some kind in employment. Thus playing a role in employment can place an individual in a better position for satisfying once ends.

Thus producing this guide for business motive and playing role in employment, can place one in a position to reflect on the motive for doing business and playing a role in employment, so as to make use of one potential and make use of available opportunities there are in our economies today. In this respect can business adventure be promoted in the economy for business and a role in employment.

INTRODUCTION

Business guide and employment role, comprise three sections. The first part look at the economic background, the way to observe the economic system, and a look at the way the economy is, both in aggregate and as well as unitary basis. Policies that are vital to control and manage the economy. Also some policies that are crucial to manage both finance and cash balances. More also what the balance of payment account is and ways for managing this balance of payment account. The contributory role of enterprise and as well as businesses is also look at. What the motivation for business is in terms of economic growth and as well in respect to human welfare. Further also the business strategies aim at economic development is also considered. The monitory institutions and the framework within which they operate is also look at. The influence of the financial institutions and as well as the collective contribution of banks is look in to as well. More also the single input of financial institutions and as the strategic aims of them is also considered. And also the aspirations of monitory institutions for wellbeing is also look in to. Further on also the market for consumer goods and services and as well as the environment that make way for operation is also look at. So also consumer behaviour and the supply of goods and services is considered. The plan of business for meeting consumer demand and for producers too is also look at. Price is also considered in relation to goods and services. The contributory role of business to market stabilisation as well as the importance for business for the operation of the economy.

The second section of business guide and employment role, look at the composite of business organisations. The consideration of business organisations in terms of their solitary nature and as well as the combination form of them. More also the formation of companies and as well as both companies limited by shares and guarantee is also look at. Further also other forms of business organisations including those of charitable nature is also considered. More also the legal framework that embodied business is also look in to. Measures for proper budgetary control and as well as consistent tax planning mechanism is considered. The concept of reporting financial performance for business and as well as the concept of proper audit practice for entities is also look at. More also ways for managing the finance of business and as the corporate aspect of management of entities is also look in to. A notion for continual assessment of business performance and as well as the style and structure of business organisation is also considered. Furthermore the principle of sustainable industrial business and the motivation for doing business is also look in to. More also the regulation of business entities and the contribution that they make towards the economy.

The third section of business guide and employment role, take a look at the role in employment. The consideration of employees and as well as for employers too in the economy is also look at. More also the contract of employment and as well as for contract for employment is also considered. Furthermore the manner of good team work and as well as the manner of good interpersonal relation is also considered. More also the manner of safe and secure work environment and as well as the manner of clean environment is also look at. The concept of a management panel and as well as a variety team managers is also considered. Furthermore the notion for continual engagement in continuing professional development programme and as well as the productivity in employment is also look at. More also the provision of benefit in employment and as well as the benefit to be in employment is look in to. So also so is the benefit of employment towards the economy.

PART ONE

PART ONE

Foreword

This section considers the economic background. The observation of the economic system. A closer look at the economy in total and as well on unitary basis. The national management policies. Method of finance management and as well as ways for keeping cash on hold. The balance of payment and as well as ways this can be managed. The contribution of enterprise in economic activity and as well as business corporation towards growth. Economic growth as a motivation for business enterprise and more also the contribution of business enterprise for welfare. The aim of business enterprise to promote welfare and also their strategic aim for economic development. The aggregate observation of the economy for welfare, together with the solitary look in the economy for wellbeing. The monitory institutions and the framework that embodied them. The influence of financial institutions and the collective contribution that banks make. The single contributions of monitory institutions and the strategic aims of financial institutions. The objectives of monitory institutions for wellbeing. The market for consumer goods and services, the environment that make way for operation and as well as a look at consumer behaviour. The consideration of supply of goods and services. Business plans aim at meeting consumer demand and as well for producers too. The price for goods and services, the equilibrium price and as well as a bargain price. The contribution of business in stabilising the market. The importance of the economic system for business and also the importance of financial institutions for business and as well as the importance of business operation for the economy and more also the importance of the market for business enterprising. The excel economy for welfare and more too an excellent business enterprising.

The Economic Background

In doing business is essential to understand the economic background within which the business framework operate. The economic system encompasses the whole business framework. As such in conducting business activities, it is thus vital to know the way in which the economy function, that embrace the whole business structure in the overall economy. In considering for instance setting and establishing a business enterprise, is thus crucial to first look in a way in which the present economic climate is at state. This in turn could lead to know how present conditions are presented in the economy. This could lead to making a right decision, as to the correct form of business structure to form, for the purpose of business venture. When the economic system is buoyant, business activities is thus attracted in entering new business ventures. Thus when the economy is doing well, business activities thus tend to increase immensely. And an increase in business activities is indeed good for the performance of the overall economy. When the economy is performing extremely, this could lead to stimulating economic growth. As the economy grow, this may present more job creation in the economy. An increase in the level of employment could lead to wealth creation in the economy. As more wealth is created, so as the improve economic well-being of the inhabitant members in the economy. This could promote the standard of living of members of the inhabitant, and lead to prosperity in the economy.

Observing The Economic System

Furthermore in the business framework, is essential to observe system in the economy, to know the trend of condition in the economy. Thus is essential to understand government policies that aim at regulating the economic system. Thus knowing policies that are in place for regulating the economic system, could lead to implementing business measures aim at promoting business operating activities. For instance to learn what specific policies affect particular type of business ventures. Knowing these policies, could lead to implementing right business strategies aim at promoting business activities. And also understanding the way particular policies do affect specific businesses, could promote planning. For instance proper planning could be made for erecting investment opportunities for business ventures. This could influence for instance what particular activities to invest in, so as to promote business activities. Investing in right business activities could yield return, and thus increase the profitability of the business enterprise. And as profitability increase, this could in turn increase growth in business operating activities for the enterprise. And this in turn could lead to opening more employment avenues in the business organisation. And as employment opportunities are created, so as increase in the overall contribution of wealth in the economy. More wealth creation is indeed could lead to overall prosperity for inhabitant members in the economy. And as such could lead to improve in the standard of living of inhabitant members in the economy. This could create more revenue in the national income of the economy.

Looking At The Economy In Total

Looking at the economy in total involve observing the behaviour of economic activities in the overall economy. In business ventures is worth pointing that in undertaking business venture activity, is necessary to look in to a feasible pattern of business operating activities in the overall economy. This would enable entrepreneur in making right decision for undertaking business venture activities, for the purpose of business enterprise objectives. The entrepreneur and business adventurers, need careful observation of the performing sectors in the wider economy, so as to identify appropriate avenues for undertaking business operational activities in the economy. Taking the initiative in committing business venture opportunities in the right performing sector, would promote fortune for the business adventurer. This in turn could lead the business performing better. And as performance improve, this in as such lead to growth in business operating activities. And as business activities grow, so is the contribution towards overall economic output in the national economy. Growth in the national economy could lead to the creation of wealth in the economy. As a consequence do prosper habitant in the national economy. An increase prosperity could drive ahead the standard of living of habitant in the national economy. This in effect could increase national income in the economy. In such a case, could lead to creation of more economic avenues in the overall economy. Thus is essential in entrepreneurship and business adventure, in taking a feasible look in to behaviours of the overall activities in the economy.

Looking At The Economy In Unitary Basis

As well as looking at the total economic activities, is also worth pointing that, observing the economy in unitary basis, so also aid business decision making. In looking for business opportunities in the economy, is as such crucial for entrepreneurs and business adventurers, to take a look at specific behaviours of economic unit activities in the economy, so as to identify opportunities for creating new business avenues in the economy. This could lead to knowing how for instance is the most performing business unit operating activities in the economy. This feasibility could enable the entrepreneur and business adventurers in making a correct decision for the creation of business avenues in conducting business operational activities in the economy. This in essence could make capital employers to be fruitful in their business adventures. And this in turn could improve the performance of business operating activities in the national economy. And also result in increase economic output in the national economy. As output increase in the national economy, so is increase in wealth in the overall economy. Wealth creation do result in improve living condition for habitant members in the national economy. Thus is vital for entrepreneurs and business adventurers, in understanding the pattern of economic behaviours on a unitary economic activity basis, so as to lead in business decision making, for the purpose of business adventures. In consequence could make the capital employer in realising increase in return from business operating activities and thus prosper entrepreneurship.

National Management Policies

In considering to enter in business ventures, is also worth to be aware of the current national management policies by the state. This consist of both fiscal and monetary policies, as are executed by the state. These policies in some way do impact on business management policies, for the purpose of business adventures. Entrepreneurs and capital employers should bear in mind the influence on these policies on their investment and as such in their decision making process. Fiscal policies are economic management strategies, that is employed by the state, in regulating economic activities in the economy, by adjustment in the national tax system, so as to conform economic behaviour to a particular pattern. For instance in booming economic sessions, the state may tend to increase taxes, so as to improve on the national income. On the other round in times of down trend economic sessions, the state may tend to lower the tax responsibility in the nation. And as such entrepreneurs and capital employers, do need inform on these policies, so as to make right business decision in their business adventures. Monetary policies are also in place by the state, aim at regulating the flow fund in the national economy. In good economic climate the state tend to set these policies, by adjusting the price for obtaining fund for investment purposes upward, thereby declining to allow too much flow of fund in the national economy. On the other way also, in down time economic condition, the state do tend to bring down the cost of obtaining fund, thereby permitting the increase flow of fund in the national economy. And as such entrepreneurs and capital employers so need to consider these policies in their investment decision making process.

Finance Management

When entrepreneur and capital employers invest in business adventures, it is important to put financial management policies in place, so as to keep the business on right pathway. Financial management do involve managing investment properly, and employing measures to put the finances of the business in to a right path. For instance in considering investment project, is worth to evaluate future outcome of the investment, thereby giving the opportunity to make a right choice on the correct project to commit capital. This should ensure that fund is utilised in the most profitable adventures. And this would increase profitability and as such yield return for capital employers. The finances of the business also need to be on the right track, so as continue engaging economic activities of the business in going basis. This may involve for instance when the finances are up, surplus funds are investment, so as to yield more return for the business. This should ensure that the profitability of the business is up. And this could lead the business in achieving growth, thereby creating more avenues for future expansion on business investment opportunities. This in turn may open doors of employment opportunities, thereby posing forward growth in the national economy. Thus is essential in business adventure, to keep a right track on the finances of the business, thereby ensuring proper financial management measures, geared for the prosperity of the business.

Cash Management

In business adventures cash management is very crucial, to ensure that proper planning is in place to make right estimate for future revenue and capital expenses, so as to ascertain the correct future cash balances at a particular time, in order to make proper planning to ensure a good flow of cash in the business stream of the adventure. And as such along in engaging in business activities, it is essential to put correct measures of these method, so as to ensure that the business is properly managed. This in turn may lead the business in to fruitful adventures. And as such the business could be in the place to engage in continuing economic operating activities. Thus a good cash flow system and liquid cash balances is indeed vital, to engage in continuing economic operating activities. Thus cash balance is essential for continuance of business. As such entrepreneurs and capital employers, do need to ensure that their cash flow system is in the right track, so as to lead them in success in business adventure. For instance managing cash well, could leave surplus fund aside, that could be used in other investment opportunities. So increase in investment opportunities, may increase the profitability of the enterprise. This in turn may also yield return for the business. As such could create opportunities for employment. Thus is very crucial for capital employers to put right measures for managing cash flow properly, so as to lead the business in prosperity.

The Balance Of Payment Account

The balance of payment account is a national account that shows the transaction effect of goods and services, imported and exported by a nation. This account thus indeed show an indication of economic performance in the overall economy. Business adventure do play a major role in improving the overall performance of this account. In the national economy, economic activities should be geared, whereby incentives are in place to encourage business activities, so as to produce goods and services, that could be exported, so as improve on this account. In this case economic output could increase, and this will leave surplus in this account. This as such could show an indication of improvement in economic activities in the national economy. Thus is vital for entrepreneurs and capital employers to engage in continuing economic activities in the national economy, so as to improve performance of economic conditions in the economy. Such activities could drive productive output, and lead to economic growth in the economy. Thus the balance of payment account could set to a surplus, and thus indicating to a better climate for engaging in fruitful business adventures. This may in turn improve the national income. Improvement in national income could open investment project by the state, and this may also create more job opportunities in the economy. In such a state, a climate is thus created, that permit business investment project to yield their return.

Managing The Balance Of Payment

The state from time on set measures in place to correct the balance of payment account. These policies are set, so as to regulate economic activities in the national economy. For instance measures may be implemented, whereby the exchange rate mechanism is used to correct the balance of payment account. In this situation for instance, if measures are employed in such that, exchange rate in the home nation is lowered in comparison to others, as such in this circumstance the goods and services produced in home nation is thus attracted to others. On the other way when such mechanism is put in place, so as to strengthening the domestic currency in order to correct the balance of payment account, in this regard foreign goods and services are attracted in the home nation. Thus entrepreneurs and capital employers and investors, do need to be aware of these measures so as aid decision making in their investment and business strategic goals. Thus business can as such take advantage of the state policies on these measures, so as to make right decisions in their investment and economic strategic goals. For instance profit from business operation do tend to increase, whereby the domestic currency is more valued than foreign currencies. As such the export of goods and services from the domestic business producers, may yield higher returns for the owners of capital. On the other way profit returns may lower, whereby foreign customers pay less in the domestic currency for producers of goods and services in the domestic currency, as such the return from the owners of capital in the domestic currency may be lowered. Thus entrepreneurs and capital employers can aid their decision making, by understanding the state policy on the exchange rate mechanism.

Contribution Of Enterprise In Economic Activity

Business enterprise do play a major role in promoting economic activity in the national economy. For instance business enterprise do engage in the production of goods and services, to meet the ends of owners of capital. This activity necessitate flow of fund through the production process. The state as whole do benefit immensely through the generation of extra levy income from revenue generated in the productive process. Also there are also job opportunities created through this productive process. This as such may promote economic output in the national economy. Thus as businesses engage in productive capacities, this may tend to promote growth in the national economy. As growth increase, this could further increase investment opportunities in the national economy. The national income could thus increase, and this may leave the state with excess to investment in more fruitful project in the national economy. Thus entrepreneurs and capital employers, also play a major role in contributing towards economic activities in the national economy. Thus economic activity can be promoted and increase in continuing engagement in production for producers of goods and services in the national economy, thereby driving overall economic growth in the national economy, and as such increase the national income.

Contribution Of Business Corporation Towards Growth

Large corporation and limited liability companies also play a major role in promoting economic growth in the economy. For instance these corporation employ large numbers of the proportion of the labour workforce. As such a high number of employment level do promote domestic growth in the economy. This can pose up the level of productive economic activity in the domestic economy. Also large corporation do engage in major investment opportunities, that tend to promote overall growth in the economy. This may lead to increase in productive output, and promote economic activity in the economy. People in the economy could be in the situation whereby they can afford goods and services of producers. Corporation also pay extra income from their revenue, as a way of statutory obligation to the state. Employers too from these organisation make share of contribution from their income to the state. This in total do generate more revenue for the state. The national income is thus increase, and do create more opportunities in government investment project. The overall economic activity in the economy is as such promoted, and this may lead to increase in economic growth in the economy. Thus large corporation and limited liability companies do contribute to a large extent, towards promoting total output in economic activity in the economy. In total these activity leads in increasing the national income in the economy. Large corporation also generate large sums of profit from their operation. This as such leave extra revenue set aside for dividend distribution, to owners of capital employed in the corporation. This is in effect increase the flow of fund in the economy.

Economic Growth As
A Motivation For Business Enterprise

Entrepreneurs and capital employers should be motivated in driving total economic growth in the economy to an upward trend. The government should promote investment opportunities in the economy, whereby entrepreneurs are encouraged to participate in continuing productive capacity in the economy. Government policies should be directed, whereby investment opportunities are encouraged in the economy, thereby promoting the overall economic activity in the economy. When investment incentives are in place, investors and entrepreneurs are encouraged to engage in productive economic activities in the economy. Incentives should also be directed towards large corporation and companies, so as to increase their participation in economic activities in the economy. In total this tend to promote growth in the national economy. An increase in growth could lead to increase in national income in the economy. As growth increase, this may also promote government investment project in the economy. The level of prosperity will also increase in the national economy. This in effect may promote the living condition of people in the nation. There would be flow of goods and services available for distribution in the economy. Fund may be readily available for investment in to profitable project in the economy. Thus stimulation by the government towards investment opportunities in the nation, could promote the overall economic welfare in the economy.

The Contribution Of Business Enterprise In Promoting Welfare

Business do have a voluntary responsibility to improve the economic welfare of habitant in the nation. In times when business enterprise is experiencing increase in return from operating business activities. It is recommended that they engage in investing in social recreational facilities, aim at promoting living condition of habitant, within their locality and region. And also within the business environment, to invest in recreational facilities, aim at promoting the welfare of staff, within their enterprise. Large corporation and companies too, should invest in recreational facilities, in the working environment, so as to promote working condition of members of staff of their organisation. Such incentive put in place by business could improve living condition both for their staff and habitant in their locality and region. For their members of staff, this could lead to incentive, that motivate them to work more productive for their organisation. And this could also make them to be efficient, thereby driving output for the organisation. This in turn may lead to increase productive output for the organisation. And an increase in output could lead to increase in profitability for the organisation. And increase in profitability could result in excess revenue being made available for distribution to subscribers of capital in the organisation. This could further result in increase in wealth for shareholders of these organisation. So also this could have an impact to drive forward productive activities in the nation. Thus is essential for business enterprise to continue to engage in recreational facilities for their members of staff, and also investing in social facilities, within their locality and region, so as to promote the welfare of habitant in their locality and region.

Business Activities Aim At Improving Overall Welfare

Business enterprise should also engage in production, by producing goods and services, aim at improving the overall welfare in society. Business enterprise should also invest in productive activities, aim at providing goods and services aim at improving the welfare in society as a whole. Investing in social welfare facilities could improve the living condition of habitant in society. As the living condition of pupils life improve, this in turn could improve their condition, whereby they participate in engaging themselves in more productive capacity, for producing goods and services for organisations. This in turn may drive productive output in upward trend. An increase in productive output, may result in increase in profitability for business enterprise. As profitability increase this may leave excess in reserve set for further investment opportunities in the nation. Employment level may go up, and there may be avenues for people seeking better employment opportunities in the nation. This could as such improve welfare in the overall economy of the nation. As employment opportunities improve, so becomes brighter prospect in the national economy of the nation. Thus business activities should also engage in fruitful social recreational facilities, so as to promote welfare of habitant in the nation. And as such thus increase the living condition of habitant in the national economy.

Business Strategy Aim At Economic Development

Businesses should set goals aim at driving the economic growth in the overall economy, so as to contribute to further economic development in the nation. Businesses should set objectives aim at increasing their economic activities. They should engage in productive economic capacity, thereby posing forward to achieve the goals of the enterprise. For every investment there should be purpose. And that objective is to strive to increase returns of the enterprise from economic operation. Increase in return is a primary objective of subscribers of capital in to a business venture. They want to be ensure that their capital investment employed in operational activities in the business enterprise do yield return, thereby achieving their main goal, for their commitment of capital in to the business enterprise. The increase in engagement of economic activities of business enterprise, could result in driving economic output in the economy, thereby contributing towards, further economic development in the economy. Further economic development leads to the creation of employment avenues in the economy. And a move in the upward trend in employment level in the economy, could lead to increase in total economic output in the economy. As economic output increase, so is the increase in national income in the economy. As national income increase, this could create further opportunities for capital investment project in the economy. As the economy give room for investment project in the economy, this could result in increase in reserve in income, available to make use of the goods and services produce by producers of goods and services. Thus business strategic objectives, can influence immensely in contributing towards further economic development in the economy.

The Aggregate Observation Of The Economy For Welfare

The economy in total should be observed so as to indentified areas in the economy, whereby economic activities can be engaged, aim at promoting welfare in the economy. Entrepreneurs and capital employers, should observe the economy in total, so as to identify opportunities in the economy, whereby investment can be committed, that leads to contributing towards promoting welfare in the economy. They should identify the goods and services that need to be produced, so as to meet the needs of habitant in the economy, that could leads to improve living condition of people in the economy. The goods and services produced in the economy, should be directed towards improving social recreational facilities in the economy, that could lead to improvement in the living standard of people in the economy. For instance individuals away from the work environment, can also be in place, whereby recreational facilities are there for the purpose of promoting social life style of individuals in the economy. Thus such activities could also result in driving total economic output in the economy. As economic output increase, so is the increase in national income in the state. Increase in national income, could increase wealth in the nation. And this could create further opportunities in the economic system of the economy. Thus participation of businesses in social investment project, could result in promoting welfare in society.

The Solitary Observation Of The Economy For Wellbeing

Investors and capital employers should observe the economy to look for those opportunities, in a particular sector of the economy, whereby capital may be employed, that leads to the production of specific goods and services, tailored to meet the needs of peculiar individuals in the economy. So also entrepreneurs and business investment, should be geared towards the production of goods and services tailored for the needs of specific individuals in the economy. This could ensure that peculiar individuals are also cared for along the productive process. This can promote economic activities and leads to increase in the production of goods and services to meet the needs of individuals in the economy. The creation of specific goods and services in the economy, could result in promoting social welfare in society. Peoples social wellbeing are as such promoted, whereby specific goods and services produced in the economy are made available to meet their needs. This as such could improve the wellbeing of individuals in the economy. And as the wellbeing of people improve, this could result in improvement in the standard of living of individuals in the economy. Thus investment opportunities created by entrepreneurs and business capital employers, could result in the creation of those goods and services tailored to meet the needs of individuals in the economy. This as a result could lead to promoting living standard and improve social wellbeing of people in the economy. This could also improve the productive capacity of the labour force. And thus lead to the efficient production of goods and services in the economy.

The Monetary Institutions

Money is the currency with which is used to obtain the goods and services demanded, so as to satisfy the needs of one, so as to meet the ends of mankind. In the modern economy today, there is the flow of unit of currency among individuals. People do engage in economic activities, that leave them with surplus cash at hand. As such for the purpose of safe keeping, there is the need to look at somewhere, to commit the safe keeping of the cash in hand. Thus monetary institutions are also the financial institutions that are established today, so as to enable the safe keeping of excess reserve in cash generated in economy, for the purpose of safe keeping. More over financial institutions accept deposit from individuals, as well as from business establishment, for the purpose to ensure safe keeping of liquid cash resources generated from economic output in the economy. There are various financial institution today in the national economies. And many are tailored to meet the needs of individuals and business establishment as well. Individuals and business establishment, want to be ensure that excess cash generated in the economy from activities in the economy, can be place to the trust of these financial institution today in the national economies. Thus financial institutions are there, to ensure the safe keeping of the excess reserve generated in the national economy. The financial institution thus facilitate activities in the economy, by ensuring that deposit can be placed with them, for the safe keeping and security of assets.

The Monetary Institutional Framework

In doing business is worth pointing that it is important to know the framework within which the financial institution in the economy operates. This could aid business activities in the economy. The financial institution operate within the framework, that permit them to accept deposit from customers, and then utilised these deposit, so as make available fund for investment project and purposes in the economy. Customers from all sectors of the economy entrust their deposit with monetary institution for safe keeping. And these institution make use of the available cash to project in to investment opportunities in national economy. In between these processes they make their return from operation. They earn extra income from projected investment opportunities in the economy, and pay back some extra income to depositors of fund, in to these institutions. The net effect therefore from these transactions, represent the return from operation of these financial institutions. They set up different financial account, tailored to meet needs of individuals in the national economy. They operate for instance current account and deposit account for both individuals and businesses at large. Deposit account do yield higher returns for the owners, than current account. Deposit account is such a type of account place at the bank, that allow long term commitment of cash asset with the banks. And this as a regard do attract a higher returns to compensate for the time value of money. Current account on the other hand, is such an account that allow fund to be withdrawn, as an when needed. And as such do not attract huge returns in comparison to savings bank account. Thus these account are maintained both for individuals and businesses alike.

The Influence Of Financial Institutions

As financial institutions are very important sectors of the national economy, the state to a some extent can influence these institution, to ensure they continue to operate within the framework for which they are set up. The state have set up a monetary institution of their own, that represent the monetary institution of the national state. This institution is also known as the central bank of the national state. The central bank act in between the various financial institutions in the economy, so as to manage the overall supply of money in the national economy. The state from time on turn to the central bank in the nation, so as to ensure that they monitor the supply of money that passes through these financial institutions in the national economy. Thus the central bank from time on influence the financial institutions in the economy, by regulating the supply of money that is allowed to flow through these institutions in the national economy. The central bank do employ such measures to ensure that they keep a track of ongoing economic activities in the national economy. Also from time on the national government, do implement policies aim at influencing, the economic activities of these financial institutions in the national economy. This is so that they can conform the direction of the economy to a particular pattern, so as to benefit the national economy as a whole.

The Collective Contribution Of Banks

In business engagement activities it is worth considering the collective contribution of the financial institutions in the national economy, towards economic activities in the economy. Banks do play a major role in speeding economic activities in the national economy. For instance they play a major part in ensuring that reserve fund is available for capital investment purposes in the national economy. They provide fund for investment purposes both for individuals and business enterprise as well. This help to increase the level of investment in economic activities in the national economy. Thus entrepreneurs and businesses can take advantage of the contribution of the financial institution in the national economy, to obtain readily available fund to entrust in their investment project. This could help speed economic activities in the national economy. As economic activities increase, this could result driving forward sum total output in the national economy. This could further create employment opportunities in the national economy. People could be in the situation, whereby they easily place themselves in employment role, in the available employment opportunities created in the national economy. This could as such make people to be better off, in terms of living condition in the national economy. Thus financial institutions play a major role collectively, in ensuring increase economic activity in the national economy, thereby posing forward the collective economic output in the national economy.

The Single Contribution Of Monetary Institutions

Monetary institutions in the national economy do play a role, in ensuring the solitary contribution to sum total output in the national economy. Banks as part of their function, do play a role in the economy, whereby they are committed to make sure they improve economic performance of economic unit in the national economy. For instance they are in the task of making fund ready for particular businesses in the national economy, so as to improve their economic performance in the national economy. As specific business unit in the national economy, is placed in the situation, whereby fund is made readily available for them, as such the opportunity is taking advantage of, to improve of their solitary economic performance in the national economy. These business unit in the national economy, can increase their economic activities in the national economy, thereby increasing their operations in economic activity in the national economy. Increase in operation from economic activity, may result increase return on the capital employed in the business. And also increase in return, may increase the profit reserve available for distribution as dividend, to the owners of capital in the business. This could lead to increase in wealth for individual investors in the business unit. Thus financial institutions play a major role, in ensuring that specific business unit in the national economy, do improve on their economic performance, thereby contributing towards growth in economic performance for these unitary businesses in the national economy.

The Strategic Aims Of The Financial Institutions

Financial institutions as part of their structure, do implement strategies, aim at driving economic growth and promote welfare in the national economy. For instance they provide counsel for businesses aim at improving their economic performance. They advice many businesses on ways to improve their performance. They also ensure they provide assistant to do to less businesses, so as to improve on their performance in the national economy. They provide them with fund, and give advice on ways to plug back the fund in their business, so as to improve their performance. These implementation by financial institutions do ensure, the revival of many low performing businesses in the national economy, thereby posing forward their economic activity, and as such improve on their performance in the national economy. As many businesses are revived in economic down turn, this as such could lead to improve sum total output in the national economy. Economic activities could increase, this could open doors of employment opportunities in the national economy. As employment increase in the national economy, so is the increase in the cash flow in the national economy. People could be in position with surplus cash, ready to obtain the goods and services to meet their needs in the national economy. Thus entrepreneurs and businesses, should take advantage of plans in place by financial institutions in the national economy, so as make ready the availability of capital, for the purpose of business investment project. Thus to an extend banks do play a role to pose up activities in the economy, by the provision of capital for entrepreneurs and businesses in the national economy.

The Objectives Of The Monetary Institutions For Wellbeing

The financial institutions in the national economy do have plans in place, whereby in their objectives are to improve the wellbeing of individuals in the national economy. Financial institution do provide services to various individuals engaged in their own activities in the national economy. Individuals are provided with services in these financial institutions, whereby they can place their surplus cash in the day for safe keeping. And also from time on easy access of their fund is made available, as and when needed. This aim as such improve the life style of individuals in the national economy, and make them happy, as their interest is promoted, and life made easy, as they go along the day in their businesses. Thus the wellbeing of individuals have improve to a some extent, through the aims of the financial institutions in the economy, geared towards promoting the life style of individual in the national economy, as they engage in the various business activities in the national economy. The aims of financial institutions as such is to make manage the account held with them by various individuals in the national economy, so as to improve their life style and as such improve on wellbeing in the national economy.

The Market For Consumer Goods And Services

The market is a place where buyers and sellers meet for the exchange goods and services produced by producers of goods and services. There are physical market location situated in many location in the national economy. In these physical locations, sellers display their goods and services for trade, and buyers check in these locations to meet their demand for the goods and services, so as to satisfy their immediate needs. Thus the market for consumer goods and services, consist of also physical locations in the economy, where the exchange of goods and services take place, between buyers and sellers. There are different varieties of market places, and form for the trade of goods and services, to be exchange between buyers and sellers. For instance in the modern economy today and with growing increase advancement in technological knowhow, opportunities is being created for instance whereby the internet and online facilities have necessitated for trade to take the form of internet and online marketing, whereby goods and services can be easily traded, to satisfy the demand for online customers. There is also the stock market in the national economy, where listed shares are traded, so as to allow capital investment to flow through listed companies easily. There are also supermarket located in different regions and sections in the national economy. More also there are town centre market location, where traders display their goods and services to be traded in the national economy. Further more in the modern economies today, the market take variety of forms, as there is increase advancement, whereby different forms of goods and services are produced to meet the needs of consumers. Thus in business is essential to know about the market, and the different form it takes, so as to identify opportunities in the economy.

The Market Environment

In doing business is very important to learn and know about the market environment. Entrepreneurs and businesses should identify areas in the market environment, where their business ventures could yield them return. Knowing about the market environment can promote business activities, improve business performance in the national economy. Entrepreneurs and businesses should undertake surveys, so as to learn more about the market environment. Analysis of these result could lead to understanding of market opportunities to take advantage of, so as to increase business activities and as such increase business performance. The market in modern economies today are becoming more dynamic, that is taking ever changing forms. As such it is important that businesses do engage in continuing learning the form of the market environment, so as make use of the available opportunities, so as to maximise returns from business operations. As the market environment is taking different forms today in the national economies, so is the need for businesses to implement plans tailored, to explore more avenues in these form of direction of the market environment. This could lead businesses to increase their economic activities, and as such improve on business performance from operations. Increase in operations may lead to increase in profit and as such yield returns for capital employed in the business.

Looking At Consumer Behaviour

In business is worth pointing that, is important to consider the pattern of consumer reaction in the market in the economy. Understanding the ways consumer react to the operation of the market forces, is thus crucial in enabling businesses to make appropriate plans, in pursuing their business goals. In business it is a good practice to know ways in which consumers react to the market forces in the national economy. Consumer behaviour implies analysing the needs and aspiration of consumers of goods and services in the national economy. That is knowing what is meant by consumer demand for goods and services. Demand in relation to the market forces, implies the immediate needs and desires of consumers of goods and services in the national economy. According to the operation of the market forces, the demand for consumer goods and services, is mainly influenced by the price to be offered in exchange for those goods and services, in need by consumers of goods and services. As such theoretically, the demand for consumer goods and services tend to go up, as the price is lowered for the exchange of goods and services, equally the demand for goods and services goes down as the price of goods and services increase. However is also worth pointing that demand may be influence in other ways by the price for goods and services. In some instances demand may tend to be elastic, especially when dealing with luxurious goods and services produced to meet the needs of consumers, for example a little change in the price brings about a large change in quantity demanded. For instance a slight decrease in price, may cause a large quantity being demanded. In this situation the effect on the marginal change in demand reaction, may lead to an increase in marginal profit. Also when there is a slight increase in price, the elasticity demand reaction, may cause a large decrease in quantity demanded. As such the marginal change in demand reaction, may lead to a marginal drop in profit. Theoretically demand may also tend to be perfectly elastic. That is demand may tend to increase and decrease at a constant price. On the other hand demand may also said to be inelastic, especially for goods and services produced aim at attracting consumers in necessary need for those goods and services, in this situation a large change in price, brings only little change in quantity demanded. So for instance a large drop in price may only cause a little increase in quantity demanded, So in this instance marginal gain may be low. Also on the other way, a large increase in price may cause only small reduction in quantity being demanded, in this circumstance also marginal return may be higher. Inelastic demand may also be perfect, that is no matter the price change, quantity demanded is at constant. Thus it is important for business to know these ways in which the market forces operates, so as to maximise returns of the business.

Considering The Supply Of Goods And Services

Business producers of goods and services also need to consider the reaction of the market forces, so as to enable them to determine the level of supply of goods and services to be made available for distribution in the market. For instance the demand for goods and services necessitate business engagement in the production of goods and services, so as to satisfy consumer demand. For instance as the quantity demanded for goods and services goes up, so is the increase supply in production of those goods and services demanded increase. Business producers of goods, as such need to keep a look at reaction of consumer demand for goods and services, so as to enable them to make available the required supply of produced goods and services, so as to satisfy consumer demand. For instance producers of goods and services may increase their return profit, as a consequence of increase in demand for goods and services. Say where demand is elastic, as for producers also their marginal profit may increase/decrease. And likewise inelastic demand may lead to drop/jump in marginal profit for producers as well. Thus is essential for business producers of goods and services to understand more ways in which the forces operate, so as to maximise their returns from operation.

Business plans Aim At Meeting Customer Demand

Businesses should aim at putting measures in place and set goals for satisfying their customers, so as to promote their sales level. Measures should be in place for improving services provided to customers, so as to increase their level of satisfaction, as a way of encouragement, for the purpose of promoting sales activities. Customer services should be tailored to the needs of individual customers, so as providing incentives for improve customary relationship, so as to improve sales activities of the business. Businesses should brand their goods and services, so as to improve the quality of the product of those goods and services. In the modern economy today, customers are increasing their choice for branded goods and services, so as to satisfy their needs. Branding can promote customer satisfaction and as such improve sales activity of the business. A business should always engage in putting plans in place for meeting the demand for their customers. For instance where the demand of customary goods and services is increasing, the business should ensure that their stock level of goods and services is adequate for meeting the needs of their customers. Thus businesses should make ways for improving their customer satisfaction and meeting their needs for goods and services demanded, so as to promote performance from business operation.

Business Plans For Producers Of Goods And Services

Business producers of goods and services as well need to put plans in place to ensure the adequate flow of goods and services in the market. They should keep a watch on the underlying trend in the market, so as to ensure the adequate flow of goods and services available to meet the immediate desires of consumers of goods and services in the market. Measures should be in the place whereby, they improve on the state and quality of goods and services supplies to the market. They should ensure the quality of goods and services are tailored to the needs of consumers of goods and services. When a product is produced, it should be tried, so as to ensure the degree of quality of the product. Such measures could ensure they supply quality product for distribution in the market. Producers of goods and services do as such play a major role in ensuring the availability of goods and services for satisfaction of customer demand. Also when the demand of goods and services tend to be increasing, they should put measures in place, to make ready the extra goods and services needed to be produced, as a result of increase in the demand for goods and services, that leads to the increase in supply. Thus as such businesses should implement strategies, to ensure the adequate flow of goods and services in the market.

The Price Of Goods And Services

The price of goods and services is the figure of amount charged to obtain the goods and services that is traded in the market. Price is the prime element in the forces of the operation of the market. Price thus influence both quantity demanded and supply. In business the correct price should be determined for goods and services to be exchanged to meet the demand of consumers of goods and services. A business can be in the position whereby at giving price, their profitability can be increased. And as such yield return to the capital employed in the business. For instance where the margin on sales price is high, this could result in increase return from operation. And as such the profit of the business may increase, due to the extra revenue generated, after the cost of generating revenue is being recovered. Likewise a business may set high mark-up on their goods and services to be traded. So in this instance where a large quantity is demanded and sales activity increased, this could lead to increase in profit from business activities. Thus a business should determine the right price, that they are willing to offer for their goods and services.

The Equilibrium Price

The equilibrium price is where the forces of demand and supply intersect, so as a price is determined at which goods and services demanded and supplied are offered. In business it is very important to determine the equilibrium price. The equilibrium price can help determine to set a correct price at which goods and services can be exchanged, so as to generate some return. The equilibrium price can assist a business to supply at a giving price, at which goods and services are demanded. Thus the equilibrium price can assist planning in setting a mark point, to determine any effect of a move in the price level offered for goods and services demanded and supplied. So a business should try to understand the reaction of any change in the move of the price level, at which they are prepared to offer the goods and services demanded. In this ways can be determine to improve the profit level of the business, so as to generate return on capital employed in the business.

A Bargain Price

In some instances where a business is not generating too much profit, ways should be determined, so as to try to ascertain a bargain price at which sales level may improve. Where sales level are down, a bargain price may be set, whereby sales level can be improved, and profitability of the business increased. In some instances a bargain price may be higher than the normal price, and in this situation, profit level may increase, where sales level are up. Also a bargain price below normal price may also be set. And where large quantities are demand and jumping up sales level, then profit may increase due to the increase level of sales quantity that offset the low bargain sales price. Thus a business should try to determine a bargain price in exceptional circumstances, so as to try to improve business performance from operation. So is very important for a business to try to set policies aim at improving the performance of the business, through the means of determining a correct price for their goods and services.

The Contribution Of Business In Stabilising The Market

Business activities can contribute tremendously towards stabilising the economic market in the economy. They can contribute through participation and engagement in economic activities aim at stabilising the economic market in the economy. They are responsible to ensure that adequate supply of economic produced goods and services are available to meet the need of the level of consumer demand in the economic market in the economy. They should monitor the trend in the demand operation, to ensure that required quantities of goods and services are produced, so as to meet the needs of the level of demand. Businesses should ensure that the price of goods and services are not rocketed, so as to avoid destabilising the market economy. Rocketed prices of goods and services can cause, and lead to inflated prices of goods and services in the market economy. Business should as such keep looking at ways whereby they can participate by maintaining the price level of goods and services in the market economy. A stable market economy can improve economic condition in the economy. As market condition improve, so is the improve condition of economic performance in the economy. This can lead to growth in employed economic activities in the economy. And as economic output increase, so is the increase economic opportunities in the economy. This can lead opening doors of employment avenues, whereby necessitating the creation of new employment opportunities in the economy. Thus businesses can play a major role in ensuring the stability in the economic market in the economy, thereby contributing towards better economic condition in the economy.

The Importance Of The Economic System For Business

The economic system is very important in the economy for business activities in the economy. Business success to an extent is very dependent on the success of the economic system in the economy. A climate of good economic system, can necessitate increase systems of business activities in the economy. As economic system improve so can as such lead to improve performance of business activities in the economy. Where there are improve economic system in the economy. This can lead to the creation of new business units in the economy, and also sustain existing business unit in the economy. New business unit established as a result of better economic system, can lead to increase in economic activities in the economy. Existing businesses as well could be in the position whereby their operational activities can be sustained, so as contributing towards improve performance in business operation. This together can lead to improving the employment level in the economy. A climate could be created where the employment level in the economy can be sustained. This can lead to increase in economic output in the economy, and as such improve performance in the economy. Thus the economic system is very important in the economy, for the contribution of sustaining business activities in the economy, thereby contributing towards good performance result for business enterprise in the economy, so as to lead in increase return of business operation to the capital employed in the business in the economy.

The Important Of The Financial Institution For Business

Financial institutions are very important for business enterprise in the economy. They play an important role in ensuring that they facilitate the activities of business enterprising in the economy. For instance banks in the economy play a major role in ensuring that they transact the business affairs of business enterprise in the economy, so as to facilitate their business operation. Financial institutions maintain bank account for business enterprise in the economy. And with these account, they provide facilities, to ensure they smooth the business activities of business enterprise, so as to contribute towards the achievement of the objectives of business enterprise in the economy. With business account held at these institutions, they facilitate receipt and payment from business activities of business enterprising in the economy. They can also contribute by putting measures to ensure that they provide overdrawn facilities for businesses, thereby making provisions for preventing the situation where fund may be insufficient to meet payments for business activities. Businesses should as such engage in putting plans to ensure that proper arrangement is in place to ensure that overdrawn facilities are in place with the bank. This for example can ensure that payment can still continue to made out of their account, even in the situation where there may be short fall in their account. Short fall in account balance may be due from delay in receipt of revenue from business operation. Thus financial institutions play a major role in ensuring that they support business operation, so as to facilitate their activities. Even in the situation whereby they can provide support through the provision of loan facilities, so as to smooth operation of business activities in the economy.

The Importance Of Business Operation For Economy

Business operation is very crucial for ensuring that their activities contribute towards improving the overall economic performance in the economy. They engage day by day in economic activities in the economy, for purpose of achieving their business goals in the economy. Businesses are daily engage in the production of goods and services to meet the demand of consumers of goods and services in the economy. These activities necessitate contributing towards total output in the economy. Businesses also do employ investment opportunities in the economy, for meeting their business purposes. They open investment opportunities in the economy, so as increase their participation in economic activities in the economy, for the achievement of the business objectives in the economy. Increase in investment by businesses, can lead to creation of new employment opportunities and also sustained existing employment level in the economy. As new opportunities for employment and existing employments are sustained, this could lead to increase in total output in the economy. This as such can lead to improve in economic conditions in the economy. As economic condition improve so is the improve performance in the overall economy. Thus business operation do play a major role in ensuring that their operation do contribute towards overall performance in the economy. So businesses as such should take advantage of these goals, so as to strive towards achievement of their business objectives, thereby improving their business performance and hence contribute towards overall performance in the economy.

The Importance Of The Market For Business Enterprising

In business enterprising the market is very essential as a prime unit for achievement of business objectives in the economy. Businesses should continually search for new ideas and inventions, thereby striving for new opportunities to maximise their performance in the market of the economy. Business should engage in continual examination of the market, so as to identify new opportunities for projecting their business operation, so as to lead to maximising their chances for improving their business performance in the economy. They should continually engage in the identification of new opportunities in the market, whereby they can take advantage of the situation and employ new capital for investment purposes in the economy. These new investment opportunities in the economy, can drive forward economic activities in the economy. This can lead to the creation of new employment avenues in the economy, thereby increasing the level of employment in the economy. This can pose forward productivity and increase total output in the economy. Also this can further contribute towards improving the economic conditions in the economy. As economic conditions improve so is improve performance in the overall economy. Thus the market is very important in the economy and a primary economic parameter and a yardstick for creating opportunities for business enterprising to achieve their business objectives, so as to meet their business goals in the economy. So businesses should make use of the opportunities of the market for maximising their chances for improve business performance and the achievement of business goals in the economy.

Excel Economy For Welfare

A sound economic system is the aspiration of the economies of the world. In every nation in the face of our planet, the aspiration of national economies of the world, is striving for the achievement of sound and excellent economic system, that create opportunities capable to meet the ends of man in the economy, thereby promoting welfare and living standard in the economy. Improvement in living standard is well connect to the total improvement in economic performance in the economy as a whole. An excellent economic condition in the economy can open opportunities for increasing economic activities in the economy. The government in the economy should strive towards contributing towards improving the economic condition of the economy. They should gear their policies aim at stimulating economic activities in the economy, thereby contributing towards improve performance in the economy. The government as well can stimulate the economy by opening investment opportunities in the economy, thereby driving forward economic activities in the economy. Incentives are necessary to set measures in place to pose forward the total output in the economy. This can lead to improve economic performance in the overall economy. The government of the economy should aspire for the achievement of sound and excellent economic system in the economy, thereby leading to improved economic performance in the economy, and as such promote the living standard and welfare in the overall economy. Thus in the economy, activities should be stimulated, so as to continue growing the economy, such that it leads to a climate of excellent economic condition in the overall economy.

Excellent Business Enterprising

A sound and excellent business enterprising is the aspiration modern entrepreneurs and capital employers today in the modern economies in the world. Entrepreneurs and businesses should strive towards the achievement of excellent enterprising that can contribute towards better economic condition in the economy. Entrepreneurs and business should set in their objectives, measures aim at striving towards the achievement of excellent business enterprising in the economy. They should make sure they engage in profitable business adventures in the economy, that can pose forward economic performance in the economy. The government in the economy as well should put measures aim at stimulating business activities of enterprising in the economy, thereby contributing towards the achievement of excellent business enterprising in the economy. The government where necessary should provide incentives for businesses aim at improving their business performance, thereby striving towards the achievement of sound enterprising in the economy. A sound business enterprise can lead to improve economic conditions in the economy. Thus as such businesses should strive towards the achievement of excellent business enterprising, that can contribute towards improve economic performance in the economy.

PART TWO

Foreword

This section considers business organisations. The solitary business organisations and as well as the combined business organisations. The formation of companies. A look at the companies limited by shares and also companies limited by guarantee. The other forms of business organisations, including charitable organisations. The business legal framework. The budgetary measures for business. A look at tax planning for business. The consideration of reporting financial performance for business. A look at the audit of business entity. Ways for managing business finance. The corporate management of business entities. More also a look at the assessment of business performance. The style and structure of business organisations is also look at. The sustainability of industrial business is also considered. The economic motivation for business and as well as the social motivation for business. The regulation of business industry is also look at. The contribution of business organisations and more also the contribution of business for economic development.

Business Organisations

Business organisations are form of enterprising that is established with the prime motive of achieving the objectives of those that may be connected with for business purposes of the organisation, and those that come in to contact with the organisation for any reason related with the affairs of the organisation. In the economies of the world today the necessities of economic activities, have made room for the need of the formation of business organisations. This is so as to provide investors and capital employers for maximising their chances in gaining return from investment opportunities for the purpose of formation of business organisations. The formation of business organisation is very important in the economies of the world today. This is so as to provide capital investors opportunities for investing, in order to enable them yield a return for capital employed in the business. The formation of business organisation also provide and create employment opportunities for individuals in the economy. Business organisations also provide opportunities for promoting social welfare in the economy. Organisations also provide a place for interaction, while along day in engagement with business activities in the economy. Business organisation do also create opportunities for establishing relationship with another along the way on employment engagement with organisation. The need for business organisation therefore is of paramount importance in the economies of the world today. As this can lead to promoting welfare in the economy and as such lead to economic development in the economy. Thus investors should engage in the business to identify new avenues in the economy, thereby finding ways for establishing new business organisational unit in the economy, so as to maximise their business potential, and yield return for their investment in the business. This could lead to increase in total economic output in the economy, and therefore increase average income level in the economy.

Solitary Business Organisation

Solitary business organisation is a form of single and sole business organisation, whereby a business unit is primarily owned and managed by the owner of the business unit. So solitary business organisations are sole business organisation, that is formed solely and managed by the owner of the business. Also sole business organisation can also be referred as sole traders engaging in business unit in the economy. An ordinary individual in the economy can rise up and decide to become say a sole trader in the economy. The sole trader organise their business unit affairs in the economy for achieving their business goals in the economy. Before the formation of single business ownership in the economy. Single traders for instance start business, by accumulating reserve income and plug it back in to the business in the form of capital employed to the business. They can also start business by say obtaining a loan for investing in to the business and repay back from the profit generated by the business. Solitary traders are responsible for managing their business and is liable for any liability associated with business. So they have no limited liability protection in relation to their business. Say for instance along their business line, the business piled up liability and is not in the position for any settlement, in this situation even to the extent of their personal possession can be sold for settlement of their liability. Solitary business organisation in the form small businesses are very essential in the economies today. Thus individuals in the economy can find new opportunities for the formation of their own business, so as to become self employed in the economy and maximise their potential from available opportunities in the economy.

Combined Business Organisations

Combined business organisations commonly known as partnership business is becoming growing line of business unit in the economies today. Partnership may take variety of forms in the economies of the world today. The basic however is the coming together of one or more individuals for the purpose of forming and doing business for the achievement of their goals in the economy. Individuals in the economy might decide to contribute capital and set up a new business in the economy for purpose of achieving their goals in the economy. There are varieties in terms of arrangement between parties in the partnership. They may for instance in their partnership agreement that parties in the partnership are to share their profit equally between themselves or they may decide to share profit in proportion to their capital contribution in the partnership business. In some partnership due to their arrangement and engagement in running the partnership business, they earn salary for participation in the business activities of the partnership. In some partnership they also make provision for providing percentage interest on the capital employed in to the partnership, according to each partners capital account balance. Thus individuals in the economy today should identify opportunities in the economy, whereby finding ways to reach their potentials by say forming and entering in to partnership business in the economy today. This is so in order to provide means for earning income through capital investment and participation in to the partnership.

The Formation Of Companies

The formation of companies may take a variety of forms in the economies of the world today. Companies may be limited by shares or say by guarantee. Companies limited by shares are limited liability companies, whose owners liability are limited to the amount of capital in the form of shares subscribed towards the share capital of the limited liability company. Also companies limited by guarantee are limited liability companies whose owners liability are limited to a guaranteed amount of share contribution towards the share capital of the limited liability company limited by guarantee. A company may be formed by say family members who wish to maximise their opportunities in the economy. A company may also be formed by groups of individual who wish to maximise their chances in the economy. In the economies of the world today there are many established companies in the economies today. There are also private companies and public companies in the economies. Public companies in the economies today create opportunities, whereby members in the economy can invest in to the company through the means of buying shares for investing in to the company. Individuals in the economies today can identify opportunities in the economy whereby they can maximise their potential through investment in to profitable companies thereby reaping their reward of shares in the company.

Companies Limited By Shares

Company formation may take the form of the creation of companies limited by shares. This form of companies make provision whereby the owners of the company liabilities are limited to the amount of share capital they contribute towards the share capital of the company. In public limited companies for example members of the public are allowed to invest in the company, by subscribing for shares in the company. Members of the public become shareholders through the purchase of shares for investment in these companies. Shares may have a normal value, that is the par value in average of the authorised share capital of the company. The authorised share capital, is the total amount of share capital that the company is allowed to raise for operation. Also the issued share capital, is the amount of share capital that the company wish to raise in the market by a way of subscription from investors in the market. Shares may be issued below their par value, so as to attract a large subscription from investors in the market. In this situation the liability of the shareholders may still be limited in proportion to the value of their shares in the company, measured at the par value in terms of their shareholding in the company. Say for instance where the company need to be rescued, investors whose shareholding have being full paid up at a discount price per shares, could lead to extra liability being outstanding to make up the difference of the shortfall in par value of their paid up share capital in the company. In limited companies there are Ordinary shareholders and preference shareholders. Ordinary shareholders is a class of shareholders that are very committed in their interest of the company. Usually they are founding members of the company.

Their shareholding entitle them to a higher dividend in the event of improve performance and increasing profit return of the company. Preference shareholders on the other hand are investors that are not prepared to take too much risk in relation to their investment in the company. They are entitled to a fixed amount of dividend from profit of the company. Thus individuals in the economy should identify investment opportunities in the economy, whereby they can make use and invest in say public limited companies, so as to provide opportunities for making return on their investment.

Companies Limited By Guarantee

Companies are also formed as companies limited by guarantee in business organisation. This type of companies are formed with the intention of protecting their members for liability of the company. Their members liability is limited by guarantee. That is their liability is limited by a guaranteed value of their shareholding in the company. This type of limited liability may protect their members in uneven circumstances only to be liable towards the company in proportion to the guaranteed amount of their shareholding in the company. Members of public can also identify opportunities for investment in to these companies thereby opening opportunities for increasing their chances of yielding return on their investment in these companies. The objectives of these type of companies tend be non-profit motive, and in most circumstances they operate in the form of charitable organisations, aim at the provision of specific services for the purpose of making no profit from their operation, also organisations in the form of association also take the form of this type of company organisations. There are limited companies by guarantee in the form of association, that is established for business operation with no motive of making profit from their operation. Thus opportunities should also be identified for the engagement with these type of entities, thereby opening employment opportunities and provide the creation of jobs and opportunities in this type of companies as well, for promoting economic development in the economy.

Other forms Of Business Organisations

There are also other forms of business organisation in the economy, that provide opportunities for investment purposes in the economy. Organisations may be set up as cooperatives for the sole benefit of their members to the cooperatives. Cooperative organisation may also vary in their activities and involvement in business. Some may be set up as financial institutions, aim at providing financial services in the market for the benefit of their members to the cooperative. They may also involve in the retail of goods and service to promote the benefit of their members in the economy. Other forms of organisations may also take the form credit union in the economy. Credit union may also be involved in the financial services market, whereby they provide financial services to promote the goals of their members to the union of the organisation. Thus individuals in the economy should also identify these organisations in the economy, where they can make use of opportunities and invest in these organisation, so as to increase their chances and earning capacity through investment project in these organisations in the economy.

Charitable Organisations

Charitable organisations are business establishment in the economy, with no motive of making profit from their operations in the economy. There are varieties of activities and involvement of charitable organisations today in the economies of the world, established for specific purposes. These organisations are formed with the purpose of engagement in activities aim at providing specific services to members in the economy, without any motive of making a profit from their activities in the economy. Individual members in the economy can identify opportunities in the economy, whereby they can participate and involve in charitable activities, so as to engage in the provision of some essential services tailored for the need of particular members in the economy for promoting economic welfare in the economy. The creation of charitable organisation in the economy can promote wellbeing for members in the economy. Members in the economy could be in the situation, whereby they can obtain some essential services in the economy at no cost to profit from business operation in the economy. The provision of such essential services in the economy, can promote life style and improve better conditions for members in the economy. Thus opportunities should also be identified in the economy, whereby the need for involvement in charitable business organisation may be identified, so as to make some provision, for engagement in activities aim at meeting some special needs of members in the economy. So the participation in these activities can promote welfare in the economy.

Business Legal Framework

In every business organisation in the economy, the business must be structured within the legal framework of business entities. The legal system have put in place guide lines for the form and structure through which business entities should operate. In many modern developed economies today in the world, business entities of any form may be required to make and file transactions and financial document to appropriate government agencies in the economy. For instance many business entities file their financial accounting result to the appropriate government agencies in the economy. The need for filing financial accounting result is very important for the government in the economy, so as to enable the appropriate government agencies to determine if any amount of tax liability is due from the operation of business entities in the economy. The filing of the financial transactions of business entities in the economy, is also important for the government, as it provide opportunity for the provision of vital information to make financial statistical analysis of performance of business entities in the economy. Thus is very important in the involvement in business organisational venture, to understand the legal framework in relation to business entities in the economy. This could ensure that they conduct their business affairs in accordance with the legal structure in place for business entities in the economy. This can help ensure that business operational activities do go on smoothly in line and in accordance with legislative guide lines by the government and legal framework in the economy.

Budgetary measures For Business

In every business entities in the economy today, budgetary measures are very important to improve the performance of the business operation in the economy. Budgetary measures implies putting the necessary mechanism in place for making sure that proper planning is in place for proposed income and revenue of the business and expected expenses and expenditure of the business operation in the economy. A business must put measures in place for implementing budgetary measures for improve performance. There should be sales, production, purchases, overhead, and as well as the master budget, for ensuring that proper mechanisms is implemented for promoting the performance of the business in the economy. The sales budget set policies to make estimate for project incomes and revenues from business operation of the organisation. The purchase budget make estimate for propose expenses on materials and associated purchases cost for supporting business operation. The production budget make estimate for propose expenses and expenditure for the cost of producing goods and services produced. The overhead budget make estimate for propose expenses and expenditure on overhead cost of producing goods and services for business activity. The master budget is the integration of the various budget, so as to determine any profit or loss on proposed and projected business operation of the business entity in the economy. Thus is very important in business organisation to make proper planning for implementing mechanisms for putting place measures to ensure that control is in place to monitor and make right estimate of proposed and projected operation of the business entity in the economy.

Tax Planning For Businesses

Tax planning is very important for business, for making provision for related tax expenses connected with business entity in the economy. Tax is a levy on income in various ways for individuals and for business entities as well in the economy. Tax enable the government in various ways to raise revenue in various forms from economic activities in the economy. The government may implement measures in the form and through fiscal policies, aim at regulating the economy through the means of the taxation policy system in the economy. So this mechanism by the government may impact in some way and affect the activities of business entities in the economy. So business entities in the economy should be aware of these policies, in order to be able to assess the tax effect of any government fiscal policy on their business operation in the economy. Being able to aware of the tax effect and impact on their business activities in the economy, can aid tax planning in their business operation. Thus business entities should make provision to ensure that proper mechanisms are in place to make sure that they implement right measures, so as to plan their propose and projected tax expenses and expenditure, so as to lead in promoting business performance of the business entity in the economy. Businesses should make proper planning for income taxes and any other related and connected taxes on business operation of the business entity in the economy.

Reporting Financial Performance For Business

Business entities should ensure that proper measures for reporting financial result of the business entity. Financial reporting involve proper record keeping of financial transactional affairs of the business entity. Business entity should ensure that proper mechanism is in place for good record keeping of the books of the financial transactions of the business entity. Proper bookkeeping should be in place to ensure that day to day transaction of the entity business financial affairs can be recorded appropriately in the ledger books of the business entity. Business entities should maintain proper bookkeeping and extract financial data transactions, for the preparation and presentation of the result of the financial affairs of the operation of the business entity. Reporting financial result of business entity involves, the preparation and presentation in the form of profit or loss account and balance sheet of the result of the financial affairs of the business entity. In international accounting standard terminology, these statement are referred to as, the statement of profit or loss and comprehensive income or expenses and also a statement of financial position of the business entity. Businesses must ensure that they report the result of the financial affairs of transaction of the business entity in accordance with recognised standard for financial reporting and also in accordance with recognised financial reporting standard, so as to ensure the appropriate and acceptable way of presentation of the financial result of the business entity. Businesses must also ensure that their financial result also take in to account the qualitative characteristics of financial data, preparation and presentation. Qualitative characteristics of financial information include, the reliability of the financial data, the faithful representation of financial information and presentation of result, the degree of comparability of financial information, the understanding of financial information by the users of financial data. These are some of the qualitative characteristics of a good financial data and information preparation and presentation. Thus is very important for business to continue ensuring the degree of quality of financial reporting of result of the affairs of the financial transactions of the business entity.

The Audit Of Business Entity

The audit of business entity is very important especially for large business entities and corporations. The audit of business entities can provide reassurance on the reliability of financial reporting and record keeping of the financial affairs of the business entity. Basically an audit is a check of the stewardship of directors of corporations. It can also be said as check on the stewardship of management of the business entity. An audit may take the form of an assurance engagement by external professional audit practitioners, who provide an independent assurance on the check of the reliability of financial reporting affairs and record keeping transactions of the affairs of the business entity. Other form of external audit engagement, may also take the form of review, whereby an external practitioner is engage in providing reasonable assurance on the reliability of financial information and transactions of the affairs of business entity. Large organisations and big corporations may also have an internal audit department, aim in looking at specific operation of the business entity. The scope of internal audit is more wider than an external audit. So internal audit focus on the operation of the business organisation as a whole, while an external audit concentrate with the operation of the financial statements of the business entity. Thus in business especially for large entities and corporations should indentify the need for the service of audit work, so as to make provision for a check on the stewardship of managers and the organisation for the benefit of the owners of the business and meeting statutory requirement of the business entity.

Managing Business Finance

Financial management is very important for business organisation. They must ensure that proper measures are in place to put the finances of the business on the right track. Managing the finances of the business is crucial in ensuring that the business be in better position to support the business operations of the entity. Where the business generate large volumes of sales activity especially on credit terms, as such proper measures should be in place to ensure that credit control policies are in place, so as to ensure good management of the finances of the business is on the right track for supporting business operations. Also especially for business that involve in international trade transactions, is very essential that they implement proper business finance management measures for ensuring the smooth finances of the business. Say for instance where a business involve in importing and exporting goods and services, they should employ financial management measures, so as to manage the threat of the business exposure to interest rate and exchange rate risk associated with international trade transactions on credit basis. Also in any involvement in business investment project, they should as well employ financial management techniques for appraising investment, so as to evaluate the out coming result of the investment project, in order to aid investment decision making of the business entity. Businesses should also identify where need may be for appropriate measures for ensuring that the business continue to refinance operation of the entity. Refinancing business may entail long term and short term financing. So the business must decide the right ways for refinancing their business where need may be, for ensuring continuing operation of the business. Thus managing business finance is of paramount importance is ensuring the continuity of the operation of the business entity.

Corporate Management Of Business Entities

Corporate management is very crucial for corporate business entities. In many modern economies of the world today, corporate management is a very essential aspect for running of the affairs of corporate business entities in the economy. Corporate management as such is the mechanism by which corporate companies are managed and the overseeing of the corporate affairs of the business entity in the economy. The need for corporate management of business arises, as a result of the agency issues faced in connection with the affairs of the business entity. An agency relationship is a connection that exist between an agent and their principal for establishment of business relation. An agent is a mediator between the principal and third parties. The agent enters in business affairs on behalf of their principal with third parties in business affairs. The need for agency relationship arise, as a result of the separation of ownership and management of the corporate company's affairs. So usually the owners of corporate companies and the management are not always the same. Thus corporate managers acting as agent of the owners of the company, are contracted for the corporate management of the affairs of the corporate business, for the purpose of the owners and stakeholders to the corporation. Thus directors are appointed to run the corporate affairs of corporate business entities for the benefit of shareholders to the corporation and connected stakeholders as well to the corporation. Usually in corporate governance shareholders appoint auditors to check on the stewardship of directors of the corporation. Corporate governance also make provision for erecting of the corporate board of directors and also the various sub-board committees as required for the corporate management of the affairs of the company. Thus corporate management is of paramount importance for corporate companies in many developed economies of the world today. As such many corporate companies should identify the need for better corporate management of the affairs of the company, so as to promote the successful management of the affairs of the corporate company business affairs in the economy.

The Assessment Of Business Performance

The assessment of business performance is of crucial importance in ensuring the continuity of business operation of the business entity in the economy. The performance of the business need to be assessed on an ongoing basis, so as to diagnose any cause for concern, in terms of the performance of the business operation in the economy. The performance of the business should be continually analysed, so as to identify ways to improve on the continuity of the business operation in the economy. The business should be continually assessed and analysed using mathematical accounting techniques and interpretation of financial data, so as to diagnose any concern in terms of business performance and operation, so as make provision for the assessment and analysis of the business, for ensuring continuity in business operation in the economy. Business performance assessment and analysis is very important, so as to identify where any need may be for any concern in the business operation, for the need to take measures for reviving the business, so as ensure continuity in business operation in the economy. Where need may be identified for reviving the business, step should be taking to find ways to project more investment in the business, so as put the business in right footing, for ensuring continuity in business operation in the economy. Assessment and analysis of the business performance, should be able to identify ways for the efficient management of working capital and long term capital investment of the business. This can help to identify ways for the efficient use of the capital resources of the business operations in the economy. Thus in business is very crucial to undertake ongoing assessment and analysis of the business operation and financial performance, so as to keep looking for cause for concern in terms of the proper management of the business operations and the efficient use of resources and investment in the business operation and financial activities of the business in the economy.

The Style And Structure Of Business Organisations

The style and structure of business organisations is of crucial importance, in ensuring good management structure and style of the business organisation. It is a good practice in business organisation to have a good style and structure of the business in place. The business organisation should be structured from top to bottom members of the organisation. There should be line of responsibility between the various members of staff of the business organisation. There should be clear line responsibility between every department in the business organisation. The structure and style of the business organisation, should be in place for the coordination of the various sections of department of the business organisation. The structure and style of business organisation, should facilitate the smooth flow of work activities between the various sections of the business organisation. Each member of staff in the business organisation, should know who to report and show responsibility for their work activities in the business organisation. In large organisations with corporate management practice in place, senior management should be accountable to the board for their work activities in the business organisation. Thus in business organisation the style and structure of the business entity is very essential for ensuring the smooth flow of work activities in the business organisation entity.

The Business Organisational Environment

In doing business is good to consider the environment in which the business organisation operate. The business organisation need to consider of the impact of their business operations to the environment in which they operate their business activities in the economy. Environmental impact is any effect of the operational business activities of the organisation may have on the environment in which the business organisation operate. The business organisation need to consider of any effect that may result from the business activities, in their operation in utilising resource input and output, along the process of supporting their business operation. They should consider the impact of the use of these resources, so as make ways for minimising any cause for concern for the environment in which the business operates. The consideration of the environmental impact on business activities, can lead to identifying ways for preserving the environment for the purpose of social habitation and wellbeing. This can ensure the need for promoting social quality life in the habitation is taking seriously, so as to promote the wellbeing of people in the environment for habitation. Thus business organisations should engage in continual assessment of the impact of their business organisational activities on the environment, thereby providing opportunities for taking measures for preserving the environment for the purpose of living habitation in the economy. Big industrial business organisations should also issue report, to show the extent to which they have manage to make effort in preserving the environment, for the purpose of promoting living habitation in the economy.

The Sustainability Of Industrial Business

Industrial business organisation should also consider in their operations, how well are they contributing towards the effort for sustainable development in the economies. Sustainability is very important for the economies of the world today. Industrial business operation should be aiming at contributing to sustainable development in the world. Sustainability is the future planning mechanism for the long term preservation of the world resources for supporting life in the planet. In sustainable planning mechanism, measures should be in place to ensure at any particular time too much the world resource is not used at any expense towards the future utilisation of those resources in the planet. So industrial business organisations should participate in the process for ensuring the preservation of the planet resource for the purpose of sustainable industrial development in the world. This should be part of the policies of business industrial organisations in the economies. Thus industrial business organisations, in their operations should gear towards to contributing for sustainable development in the economies.

The Economic Motivation For Business

In business organisation is worth pointing to consider the economic motivation for doing business. Many business organisations primary motive is for the making of profit from their operation. The business engage in activities for the realisation of profit for doing business. This profit motive serve as a interest in participation of business activities in the organisation. Also other economic reasons for doing business is for the creation of jobs and opportunities in the economy. The establishment of business organisation, leads to the creation of jobs and opportunities for people in the economy. Shareholders also who invest in businesses expect some return for their stake in the business from operation. As the business make some profit from operation, this may leave extra reserve available for distribution in the form of dividend to the shareholders of the business organisation. Dividend payment to shareholders can increase their wealth, and put them in better position for projecting new investment opportunities in the economy. So also the economic contribution of business organisation is the provision of employment opportunities for people in the economy. This creation of employment opportunities for people, can lead promoting their material welfare in the economy. They may be in the position to afford the goods and services produced in the economy, so as to promote their wellbeing in the economy.

The Social Motivation For Business

The social motivation for doing business in this regard, refers to the no profit motive for doing business. That is doing business with no profit motive from operation. Business organisation in the economy may be established with no profit motive in the economy. The benefit of these organisation is to tailor some essential social services to meet the needs of individuals in the economy. So the purpose is the provision of essential services to meet the needs of individuals in the economy. Although the organisation is run with no profit motive, yet it provide benefit by way of promoting welfare and creating jobs and opportunities, along the business operation in the economy. Thus businesses can also engage in not for profit activities in the economy, thereby promoting wellbeing in society and provide the opportunity for the creation of jobs and opportunity for people in the economy. This can lead to improvement in economic and social condition in the economy.

The Regulation Of Business Industry

In doing business is worth to know that certain business industries are regulated, so as to manage the economy properly. The government from time on do put measures in place, for the regulation of business industries in the economy. The regulation of business industry is the intervention by external organisations, aim at structuring particular type of business industry to conform to a pattern, that leads to the benefit of the economy as a whole. The government may set up organisations in the economy, for the main purpose of regulating certain type of business industries in the economy. There are other independent regulating business bodies, form for the purpose of regulating particular type of business industry in the economy. Thus business organisation in the economy, should be aware of regulation that may be in place that affect the operation of their business. Regulation is essential in order to shape the operation of certain industries in the economy. This can ensure that particular businesses do not dominate the market through their operation in the economy. Regulation can also make business industries operate in accordance to strict business pattern in the economy.

The Contribution Of Business Organisation

Business organisation in the modern economies of the world today, have contributed tremendously towards promoting social welfare in the economy. Business organisations are engaged in the production of those goods and services needed for meeting the needs of individuals in the economy. They promote wellbeing by engaging in the production of goods and services needed for people in the economy. The creation of essential goods and services by business organisations, can lead to promoting the wellbeing of individuals in the economy. People living standard can be improved, whereby goods and services are made available, for meeting their immediate needs in the economy. Business organisation also engage in the creation of essential services in the economy aim at promoting social welfare in the economy. The provision of essential services for welfare, can lead to the promoting living condition for people in the economy. Thus business organisations have contribute extremely towards promoting the life style of people in the economy.

The Contribution Of Business For Economic Development

Business organisations in the economies of the world today have also contribute tremendously towards the economic development in their economy. Business organisation are responsible for creating investment opportunities in the economy. They also create employment avenues in the economy. Business organisations are responsible to facilitate the flow of economic activities in the economy. The investment opportunities in business organisation, provide return to investors on their capital employed in the business. This help to promote income level in the economy. And also the creation of employment opportunities by business organisation, do promote the income levels of individuals earning capacity in the economy. This increase in income level in the economy, can lead to increase in wealth for individuals in the economy. They may be in the position to afford the goods and services produced in the economy. This can as such drive productivity and increase total income level in the economy. Thus business organisations have contribute extremely towards economic development, through their participation in economic activities, for the benefit of the economy as a whole.

PART THREE

PART THREE

Foreword

This section looking at the employment role, employees in the economy and as well as employers in the economy. The contract of employment engagement and also the engagement for contract for employment. The manner of good team work is also look at. And more also the manner of good interpersonal relation and also the manner of safe and secure environment and as well as the manner of clean environment. The management panel is considered. And also as well a variety of team managers is also look at. The engagement in continuing professional development programme is considered too. The productivity in employment as well is look at. More also the provision of benefit in employment is considered as well. Further too the benefit of engaging in employment role and as well as the benefit of employment in the economy.

Employment Role

Employment role is the participation in work related activities for the purpose of engagement in productive services for an employer, in any form of business organisational entities, whether private sector employment or public sector employment, or may it be in not for profit organisations or say charitable organisations and trust in the economy. Almost in all economies of the world the aspiration of individuals is to engage in gainful employment role, any form in economic activities in the economy. Taking up an employment role, can enable an individual to increase their earnings potentials in the economy. Earning income through employment opportunities in the economy, can promote the wellbeing of the individual and increase the income capacity on the individual in the economy. The government can also benefit from the employment of an individual, through the means of tax collection from the earnings of the individual in the economy. As individuals in the economy earn their income through gainful employment opportunities in the economy, this can help increase the income levels in the economy. People living life styles and conditions can also be improve, through the way of earning income, by way of gainful employment opportunities in the economy. Individual social wellbeing can also be promoted, whereby they may in the position to meet their needs in the economy, so as to improve their life style and living condition in the economy. Thus taken up an employment role is of valuable importance, as it can lead to improving life style and living conditions of individuals in the economy.

Employees In The Economy

An employee is someone that engage in gainful employment for an employer in an employment role in any business organisational capacity. People engage in gainful employment by providing services in return for an income through the connection with in any business organisational capacity in the economy. Employees in the economy secure various roles in business entities in the economy. There is a scale of earning capacity in employment roles in the economy. Some jobs in the economy attract higher wages or salary in return for services with an employer. The degree of the extent of earning capacity, depend on the type of skills, ability and qualification demanded for the employment role in the economy. For example a higher scale job in business industries in the economy, may require a talented employee with the right skills and abilities to participate in the employment role in the economy. Also lower grade employees in the employment role in the economy, may not be required to possess higher level skills and talent for performance of their duties in an employment role in the economy, as in most cases ongoing training can be provided to enable the employee to perform their task well in the employment role in the economy. So there are higher grade employees with talent and skills, that attract higher wages or salary and lower grade employees that not need much talent and skills in doing their job and as such are lower scale income earners in employment role in the economy.

Employers In The Economy

An employer is someone who take on an employee for the purpose of engagement in the provision of services required in production. An employer may be responsible for taking small or large number of employees for the engagement in productive work in the economy. Employers in the economy create doors of opportunities in employment role in the economy, so as to participate and increase the level of economic activities in the economy. Employers may be private industry employers or public industry employers. They may be employers from the business sectors in the economy or say business sector employers with no profit motive in their objectives in the economy. During improving economic conditions, employers tend to take on more employees from the workforce in the economy. And also in times of uneven economic conditions, they tend to scale down their operation by not taking on too much employees from the workforce in the economy. Projection of investment opportunities in the economy do provide an incentive for employers in the economy take on more employees from the labour workforce in the economy. The government in the economy also participate in improving the employment level in the economy, through the projection of investment opportunities in the economy. The national government may also tend to implementing policies and mechanism in the economy, that aims at promoting the level of employment opportunities in the economy. Thus employers in the economy should be encouraged to take on more employees in employment role in the economy, thereby promoting wellbeing for individuals and as such contribute to increasing income levels in the economy.

Contract Of Employment

In seeking gainful employment opportunities in the economy, employers engage employees in a contract of employment. A contract of employment is the creation of employment opportunity, that make provision for the engagement of an employee in an employment role for continuing engagement in the provision of services for an employer. In a contract of employment the employer is responsible for the work related matters of the employee. The employer specify the task and duties of the employees as set out in the contract of employment engagement letter, and also the manner in which the employee is engage in an employment role with the employer. In a contract of employment the employer is responsible for welfare of the employee at work. The employer provide all the necessary services to facilitate the operation of the employee in the employment role with the employer. In contract of employment the employer specify the pay scale of the employee. The letter of engagement stipulate, the pay rate, and all other associated employment benefit entitlement with the employer in the employment role. The employer is responsible to follow procedures to ensure any amount due in respect of pay as to you earn deductions, are allowed for, and provision made for any PAYE deductions from the employee in the employment role. Thus contract of employment make provision for engaging individual employees in gainful employment role, so as to contribute in fulfilling the business objectives of the employer in the employment role.

Contract For Employment

Contract for employment is the engagement in employment related role without gaining employment directly from an employer. Individuals in the economy may decide to become self-employed. That they establish themselves to be responsible for employment related obligation. Self-employed do business, through gaining contracts from employers, for undertaking productive work for the employer. Self-employed are responsible for providing their work related tools, for the performance of their contract for services. They are responsible to account for their business affairs separately. They may be in engagement in contract for service for different employers. Each individual employer is represented as client to the self-employed business. As such they do business with many client in their list of business client. Self-employed in the economy may also be involve in hiring their staff to support their business. In this respect they are responsible to manage the work related affairs of that they have hired. The situation would as in the case of any ordinary employer in an employment role. So individual in the economy should identify opportunities in the economy, whereby they participate in business related employment role, by way of being self-employed in the economy. Self-employment can open employment opportunities for engagement in an employment role, for purpose of generating and earning some income from the self-employed business in the economy. Self employment is very important in the economy, as it can help improve the level of employment in the economy. And this can promote income level in the economy, and pose up the earning potential of individual self employed in the economy.

The Manner Of Good Team Work

In the workplace the manner of good team work is of importance, to ensure that work system do flow in the organisation, so as to facilitate the business of the organisation. Members of employment workforce in an organisation should team up together, and work in the atmosphere of good team work in the organisation, so as to smooth the business of the organisation. Members of staff of the organisation in every department should promote the work process in the organisation, by way of working towards the achievement of the same goal for the organisation. Members of staff should together do strive to achieve the goals of the business organisation. This will help to promote the flow of the work process in the organisation, thereby increasing the opportunity for making the business to achieve the goals of the organisation. Thus the manner of good team work is essential for ensuring that work related business flow in good manners to facilitate the business of the organisation. This can help co-ordinate the flow work in every section of the organisation, thereby striving for fortune of the business organisation. So a manner of team work can facilitate the work process in organisations. Thus is important in employment roles in an organisation to follow the pattern of good team work so as the smooth the flow of the work process in the organisation.

The Manner Of Good Interpersonal Relation

The manner of good interpersonal relation is also important to facilitate the work process in the organisation. Individual employees in the organisation need to develop good interpersonal relation, so as to facilitate the smooth flow of work in the organisation. Interpersonal relation requires individual employees to the develop the attribute of interpersonal skills, that can put them in better shape to deal with colleagues in the work place, so as the smooth the flow of work in the organisation. Interpersonal skills can be developed by way opening up oneself for another, so as allow an atmosphere to interact with another. This essential skills developed by an employee, can produce interpersonal skills, capable of dealing with another in the work place in good relation, so as to smooth the work process in the organisation. Thus a manner of good interpersonal relation is of paramount importance in the work place, so as to help in the process to establish a good link with one and another in the work place, thereby facilitating the work process in organisation. Interpersonal skills can promote individual in employment role in an organisation. This can ensure the continued engagement in employment role in an organisation. So individuals in employment should practice the exercise to establish good interpersonal relation with another in the work place, so as smooth the flow of work in the organisation.

The Manner Of Safe And Secure Environment

In the organisation, policies should be in place to ensure a safe and secure work environment in the workplace. The organisation should find ways for ensuring safety and security in the workplace of the organisation. The organisation should set priority of the continued engagement in the process of this task, to ensure safe and secure workplace in the organisation. A safe and secure workplace in the organisation, can facilitate the flow of the work process in the organisation. This can lead to a system of smooth working environment in the organisation, whereby the work process in the organisation is geared for progress in accordance with the agenda of the organisation. Every member of staff in the workplace of the organisation, should strive towards the achievement of this goal in the organisation's agenda. All members of the employment workforce in the organisation, should participate towards this process, and engage in continuing involvement to strive achieving this objective of the organisation. Ensuring a safe and secure workplace in the organisation, entails setting health and safety policies, aim at identifying ways in the workplace, for which priority can be set, for ensuring a safe and secure workplace, so as to smooth the work process of the organisation, thereby promoting the welfare of members of staff in the organisation. Thus the organisation should consider safety and security in the workplace more important in the organisation's planning system, so as to make ways to prioritise this process in the workplace, thereby contributing to the smooth deliver of work processes in the organisation.

The Manner Of Clean Environment

Similarly the organisation should also consider ensuring a clean working environment in the workplace of the organisation. In every working day in the calendar year, the organisation should ensure the workplace is clean and conducive for engagement in the working practices of the organisation. Every day of the week, is should be manner of routine process, for cleaning the working environment in the organisation. Dedicated members of staff should be assigned to doing this process in the organisation. The organisation should specify the manner of the task, and should encourage the continued delivery of this task in the workplace of the organisation. In large organisations a team of staff should be elected for the delivery of this process in the organisation. Where there is a big cleaning team, the taskforce should be controlled by a team controller, that aims at overseeing the process of the operative cleaning taskforce in the organisation. The organisation should take this process important, so as to ensure the manner of clean working environment in the organisation. This mechanism should be part and parcel of the organisation's planning taskforce in the organisation. Priorities most be in place to ensure the continued delivery of this process in the workplace of the organisation. The organisation should continually observe this process in the workplace, thereby ensuring the smooth delivery of this task in organisation. Thus a manner of clean working environment is paramount for the workplace in the organisation, as this can lead facilitate the smooth delivery of work process in the organisation.

The Management Panel

In business organisation is worth to consider the management process of the organisation. The management process in business organisation is crucially important, to ensure the success of the business of the organisation. They should consider business management a priority in the organisation's planning process. Business management can ensure success in the progress of the organisation. In every organisation a management must be in place, to oversee the management of the business organisation. A successful business lies in good management of the organisation. The organisation should set objectives and taskforce to engage managers in successful conduct of business affairs of the organisation. Is recommended that in business organisation, a panel of managers should be set up, whose taskforce is to ensure the successful conduct of the business affairs of the organisation. The panel of managers should assemble themselves, whereby they engage in the proper planning process of business affairs of the organisation. This panel of managers should set target for strategic management of the business affairs of the organisation. This panel of managers from time on should continue engaging in the process of proper strategic planning of business organisation. Managers should work together to strive to achieve the objectives of the business organisation. Thus a business organisation should consider in their agenda for need to continue engage the collective management officers of the business organisation, thereby working towards the achievement of goals of the organisation.

A Variety Of Team Managers

In business organisation is also worth pointing that is essential to engage different sets of team managers, so as to strive towards the proper management of business organisation. Engaging managers in different groups can aid the decision making process of the organisation. Various team group of managers should be in place, that aims at the collective contribution of the decision making process of the organisation. The various team of managers in the organisation should engage in considering the specific management of the various issues affecting the business of the organisation. The team of managers should set strategic goal to strive towards the achievement of overall goals of the business organisation. Managers play a major role in the business management of organisation, for the purpose of ensuring good conduct of the business affairs of the organisation. So engaging different sets of managers in variety of groups in the organisation, can aid the planning process of the organisation. This teams should be gear towards looking at specific ways to promote the success of the business organisation. The managers in organisation's may have different work experiences, and as such the collective engagement of them, can ensure they consider for good the better management of the organisation. Thus engaging managers in the organisation, can contribute towards proper planning and aid the decision making process of the organisation. So this can lead to promoting the success of the business organisation.

The Engagement In Continuing Professional Development Programme

Employees in employment role in an organisation should engage in continuing professional development programme, so as to continue improving their work performance in the organisation. Continuing professional development programme, implies identifying the need to improve on skill, through further training and learning to acquire new skills, so as improve on performance in an employment role in a business organisation. The engagement in continuing professional development programme can improve the work performance of an individual, and contribute a more better way of doing work, in an employment role in a business organisation. Continuing professional development programme may entail, acquiring new skills and talent, may it be through embarking on further education and training or through the engagement of work related experiences and learning process, geared to contribute towards improve performance in work processes in an employment role, in a business organisation. This can lead to the development of improve skills and talent for individuals, through experience in learning process, aim at improved work performance in an employment role with a business organisation. Thus a business organisation should encourage their members in an employment role with the organisation, to continue in the engagement for improving their work performance, through the participation in continuing professional development programme, by way of learning experience aim at contributing for the delivery of improve work performance for their business organisation. So a business organisation should encourage their members in an employment role, to improve their work performance, by way of engagement in continuing professional development programme for the delivery of better work performance in the business organisation.

Productivity In Employment

Business organisation should make use of the opportunity to make their members in an employment role with the organisation to be productive, for purpose of making the business to be more successful. The business should identify ways in which they can contribute to make their members of the employment workforce to be productive for the business organisation. Incentives should be provided aim in driving forward the productivity of their workforce in the organisation. The business should able to recognise the need of their workforce, so as to identify, the means by which they can be supported, so as to improve their productivity for the organisation. They can for instance contribute to improving the performance of their workforce, by a way of encouragement capable to drive the workforce in doing their work more better, for the business organisation. Encouragement can also be provided by way of recognising the contribution of the workforce, and having sense of value for the effort of the workforce, towards their contribution in work performance for the business organisation. The business should also take measures for encouraging their workforce to show and have keen interest in the work process in the business organisation. This can lead to improvement in work performance in the business organisation. So business organisation should make use of opportunities and recognise the need to participate in the process of continued encouragement of the workforce, for improve performance in the work process in the business organisation.

The Provision Of Benefit In Employment

Business organisations should attract members of the labour workforce to their organisation, by designing employment packages, so as to attract well performing staff to their organisation. Employment packages should design, such that it include the necessary benefit in kind, capable to attract well performing of the labour workforce to their organisation. Benefit in kind may include, the provision of work related retirement income, a health insurance cover, expense reimbursement, holidays, refreshment services. This can lead to attracting better performing members of the employment labour workforce to their business organisation. This can also encourage potential members in employment role with the business organisation, to aspire to work for the business organisation. This can also help the retention of potential members in an employment role, to have long term employment ambition with the business organisation. This can enable potential members of the workforce to strive to gain role in employment with the business organisation. Also the business should also strive to design such packages both for existing and potential members of workforce of the business organisation. This can ensure that incentives are provided for the encouragement of members of their workforce to perform more well for the business organisation. This can contribute and make the workforce to strive more better, for smooth delivery of work performance of the business organisation. Thus the provision of benefit in employment, by way of benefit in kind, can contribute to improve work performance of members of the workforce with the business organisation. This as such can lead to successful performance of the business organisation.

The Benefit Of Engaging In Employment Role

There are tremendous benefit for engagement in employment role in business organisation. Individuals in the economy, can benefit extremely through gainful employment opportunities in the economy. Employment opportunities for individual in the economy, can open many doors of opportunities for the individual in the economy. Individuals in the economy in employment role in the economy, employment can open doors of opportunity for the individual in the economy. The individual can be placed in the situation, to earn themselves higher income, through gainful employment opportunities in the economy. This can increase the income level of the individual in the economy. They may be in the situation to improve their life style and living condition in the economy. They may in the position to meet their needs for the goods and services, that is necessary to improve their life style and living condition in the economy. Gaining employment can also provide security in terms of income and be in the position to be able to plan for retirement, thereby providing assurance for guaranteed income in future retirement period in the economy. Employment role can also promote the social life style of the individual in the economy. Individual in the economy can place themselves, where through gainful employment in the economy, they can promote relationship with another, through personal friendly interaction in the workplace, thereby promoting the social life style of the individual in the economy. Thus employment opportunity in the economy, can provide means for improve income earning capacity and the promotion of social life interaction in the economy.

The Benefit Of Employment For The Economy

The benefit of employment for the economy is enormous. There are numbers of benefit of employment for the economy. The creation of opportunity for employment in the economy, can contribute towards increase income levels in the economy. This increase income level in the economy, may lead increase in spending level in the economy. As income and spending level increase in the economy, so is the increase movement in the economic process in the economy. This can lead to improve performance in economic condition in the economy. The creation of employment opportunities in the economy, can also provide opportunity for the government to raise some revenue from the creation of the employment opportunities in the economy. This can provide means for the government to raise more income in the economy, by way of the creation of employment opportunities in the economy. The indication is that as the level of employment level increase in the economy, so is the increase in total output in economic performance in the economy. This can lead increase in the growth rate of the economy, and improve performance for the economy.

www.ingramcontent.com/pod-product-compliance
Lightning Source LLC
Chambersburg PA
CBHW030838180526
45163CB00004B/1364